THE
BIBLICAL
ELDERSHIP
BOOKLET

Restoring the Eldership to Its
Rightful Place in the Church

REVISED

———

Alexander Strauch

Lewis & Roth Publishers

P. O. Box 469, Littleton, CO 80160

About the Author:
Alexander Strauch has served in the leadership and teaching ministry of Littleton Bible Chapel (near Denver, Colorado) for nearly 50 years. As a gifted Bible teacher and church elder with extensive practical experience, Mr. Strauch has taught in more than 25 countries and has helped thousands of churches worldwide through his expository writing ministry. He is the author of *Biblical Eldership, Meetings That Work, Agape Leadership, Men and Women: Equal Yet Different, The Hospitality Commands, Leading with Love, Love or Die, If You Bite & Devour One Another* and *Paul's Vision for the Deacons.* These books have been translated into over 30 languages. In recent years, he has also made an impact on churches around the world through the ministry of BiblicalEldership.com.

Biblical Eldership Booklet
ISBN: 0-93608-315-8
© 1987, 1997 by Alexander Strauch. All rights reserved.

This booklet is an abridgment of *Biblical Eldership: An Urgent Call to Restore Biblical Church Eldership* by Alexander Strauch.

Cover Design: Stephen T. Eames (EamesCreative.com)
Editors: Stephen and Amanda Sorenson

All Scripture quotations, except those noted otherwise, are taken from the New American Standard Bible®, Copyright 1960, 1962, 1963, 1968, 1972, 1973, 1975, 1977, and 1995 by The Lockman Foundation. Used by permission.

Printed in the United States of America
Nineteenth Printing / 2018

To receive a **free catalog** of books published by Lewis & Roth Publishers, email info@lewisandroth.com or call toll free: 800-477-3239. If you are calling from outside the United States, please call 719-494-1800.

Lewis & Roth Publishers
307 Delaware Dr.
Colorado Springs, CO 80909-6614

The Problem

———

While attending a sacred music concert, I received an insightful lesson in ecclesiology.[1] As I walked into the main foyer of the church where the concert was being held, I immediately noticed the photographs and names of the senior pastor and his staff arranged in a pyramid within a glass encasement. The senior pastor's photograph was at the top, his three associate pastors' photographs were below, and the rest of the church staff's photographs completed the base of the pyramid. As I walked further into the building and down a side hall, I saw another glass encasement that contained the photographs and names of the church elders. I immediately thought, *What a superb illustration of how the church elders have been pushed aside to a scarcely visible position in the church!* This is quite different from the New Testament model of eldership.

My first encounter with church elders occurred when I was a young teenager preparing for confirmation. During confirmation classes, I told the minister about my conversion to Christ, which had taken place the previous summer at a Bible camp. He was so intrigued by my youthful, exuberant testimony of Christ that he asked me to share my story with the church elders. So I met with the elders and told them about my new relationship with Jesus Christ. They sat speechless, looking totally puzzled. I was saddened by their response because I realized that they didn't understand what I was saying. That experience left me with little confidence in the elders or the church.

My next encounter with church elders, however, was altogether different. While attending college away from home, I was invited to a church that taught and practiced authentic biblical eldership. The elders of this church took seriously the New Testament commands for elders to be biblically qualified and to actively pastor the flock of God. They provided strong leadership, loving pastoral care and discipline, sound Bible teaching, and humble, sacrificial examples of Christian living. As a result, they were highly esteemed by the church. The inspiring example of these men first awakened in me a positive interest in the subject of church eldership.

Later, while attending seminary, my growing interest in eldership was vigorously challenged. During a class on church polity,[2] which stubbornly resisted any notion of an elder-led church, I asked the professor, "But what do you do with all the scriptural texts on elders?"

He quickly responded, "Numbers of texts on elders mean nothing!"

I thought, but didn't have the nerve to express it publicly, *Well, what does mean something? Your nonexistent texts on clerics?* This and other similar experiences served only to stir my increasing conviction that eldership was a biblically sound doctrine that most churches either ignored or misinterpreted.

Several years later, I was preparing a series of sermons on the doctrine of the Church. When I came to the subject of eldership, I was shocked to discover that there was no full-length book on the subject. There were small booklets, journal articles, and chapters within books, but no thorough treatment of the subject from an expository viewpoint. This lack of exposition was hardly believable, especially when I considered the elders' primary role as leaders in the first churches and the number of scriptural texts devoted to elders. It finally ignited my desire to write on the subject of eldership.

I don't believe any doctrine of Holy Scripture should be neglected or defined out of existence. Yet this is precisely what many churches have done to the biblical doctrine of eldership.

Even among churches that claim to practice eldership, elders have been reduced to being temporary, lay, church board members, which is quite contrary to the New Testament model of pastoral eldership. Although such churches may have an eldership, it is not a biblical eldership.

Literally tens of thousands of churches worldwide practice some form of eldership because they believe it to be a biblical teaching.[3] Unfortunately, because the advocates of eldership have been so terribly delinquent in adequately articulating this doctrine, a great deal of confusion and unbiblical thinking surrounds the topic among most elder-led churches. There are persistent, crippling misconceptions about eldership that hinder churches from practicing authentic biblical eldership. This subject is too important to the local church to be bogged down in confusion and error.

To help remedy this appalling confusion over eldership, I wrote *Biblical Eldership: An Urgent Call to Restore Biblical Church Leadership*. This book was aimed primarily at churches that practice eldership but may misconstrue its true biblical Christian character and mandate. This booklet briefly summarizes *Biblical Eldership*. Hopefully it will whet your appetite to read the entire book, but more important, it will motivate you to study further the biblical teaching on eldership. Precious truths, no doubt, still await discovery.

Biblical Eldership Defined

Despite what all the New Testament communicates, the doctrine of biblical eldership has been sorely misunderstood.

Even churches that claim to be governed by a plurality of elders have redefined eldership so that its original purpose and noble standing have, in practice, been eclipsed by the ordained pastor and his staff. To clarify biblical eldership in light of contemporary church practices, I present the following five, distinguishing features of a New Testament, Christian eldership: pastoral leadership, shared leadership, male leadership, qualified leadership, and servant leadership.

Pastoral Leadership

When most Christians hear about church elders, they think of an official church board, lay officials, influential people within the local church, or advisers to the pastor. They think of elders as being policymakers, financial officers, fund-raisers, or administrators. I call these types of elders "board elders." People don't expect "board elders" to teach the Word or be involved pastorally in people's lives. Victor A. Constien, a Lutheran official and author of *The Caring Elder,* illustrated this popular view of the elders' role when he wrote, "Members of a congregation's board of elders are not assistant pastors. They *assist* their pastor . . . elders help facilitate and strengthen the working relationship of the church staff."[4]

Such a view, however, not only lacks scriptural support but flatly contradicts New Testament Scriptures. A person doesn't need to read Greek or be professionally trained in theology to understand that the contemporary, church-board concept of eldership is irreconcilably at odds with the New Testament definition of eldership. According to the New Testament, elders lead the church, teach and preach the Word, protect the church from false teachers, exhort and admonish the saints in sound doctrine, visit the sick and pray, and judge doctrinal issues. In biblical terminology, elders shepherd, oversee, lead, and care for the local church.

Therefore, when Paul and Peter directly exhort the elders to do their duty, they both employ shepherding imagery. *It should be observed that these two giant apostles assign the task of shepherding the local church to no other group or single person but the elders.* Paul reminds the Asian elders that God the Holy Spirit placed them in the flock as overseers for the purpose of shepherding the church of God (Acts 20:28). Peter exhorts the elders to be all that shepherds should be to the flock (1 Peter 5:2). We, then, must also view apostolic, Christianized elders to be primarily pastors of a flock, not corporate executives, CEOs, or advisers to a pastor.

If we want to understand Christian elders and their work, we must understand the biblical imagery of shepherding. As keepers of sheep, biblical elders are to protect, feed, and lead the flock and to help meet the flock's many practical needs. Using these four, broad, pastoral categories, let us briefly consider the examples, exhortations, and teachings of the New Testament regarding shepherd elders.

Protecting the Flock: A major part of the New Testament elders' work is to protect the local church from false teachers. As Paul was leaving Asia Minor, he summons the elders of the church in Ephesus for a farewell exhortation. The essence of Paul's charge is this: *guard the flock—wolves are coming:*

> And from Miletus he sent to Ephesus and called to him the elders of the church. . . . "*Be on guard for yourselves and for all the flock,* among which the Holy Spirit has made you overseers, to shepherd the church of God which He purchased with His own blood. I know that after my departure *savage wolves will come in among you,* not sparing the flock; and from among your own selves men will arise, speaking perverse things, to draw away the disciples after them. *Therefore be on the alert.*" (Acts 20:17, 28-31; italics added).

According to Paul's required qualifications for eldership, a prospective elder must have enough knowledge of the Bible to be able to refute false teachers:

> For this reason I left you in Crete, that you might set in order what remains, and appoint elders in every city as I directed you, namely, if any man be above reproach . . . holding fast the faithful word which is in accordance with the teaching, *that he may be able . . . to refute those who contradict* [sound doctrine] (Titus 1:5, 6, 9; italics added).

The Jerusalem elders, for example, met with the apostles to judge doctrinal error: "And the apostles and the elders came together to look into this [doctrinal] matter" (Acts 15:6). Like the apostles, the Jerusalem elders had to know the Word so that they could protect the flock from false teachers.

Feeding the Flock: Unlike modern, church-board elders, all New Testament elders were required to be "able to teach" (1 Tim. 3:2). Listing elder qualifications in his letter to Titus, Paul states, "[The elder must hold] fast the faithful word which is in accordance with the teaching, that he may be able both to exhort in sound doctrine and to refute those who contradict" (Titus 1:9). In an extremely significant passage on elders, Paul writes about some elders who labor at preaching and teaching and thus deserve financial support from the local church:

> Let the elders who rule well be considered worthy of double honor, especially *those who work hard at preaching and teaching.* For the Scripture says, "You shall not muzzle the ox while he is threshing," and "The laborer is worthy of his wages" (1 Tim. 5:17, 18; italics added).

Paul reminds the Ephesian elders that he has taught them and the church the full plan and purpose of God: "For I did not shrink from declaring to you the whole purpose of God" (Acts 20:27). Now it was time for the elders to do the same. Since elders are commanded to shepherd the flock of God (Acts 20:28; 1 Peter 5:2), part of their shepherding task is to see that the flock is fed God's Word.

Leading the Flock: In biblical language, to shepherd a nation or any group of people means to lead or govern (2 Sam. 5:2; Ps. 78:71, 72). According to Acts 20 and 1 Peter 5, elders are to shepherd the church of God. So, to shepherd a local church means, among other things, to lead the church. To the church in Ephesus, Paul writes, "Let the elders who rule [lead, direct, manage] well be considered worthy of double honor" (1 Tim. 5:17). Elders, then, are to lead, direct, govern, manage, and otherwise care for the flock of God.

In Titus 1:7, Paul insists that a prospective elder be morally and spiritually above reproach because he will be "God's steward." A steward is a "household manager," someone with official responsibility over the master's servants, property, and even finances. Elders are stewards of God's household, the local church.

Elders are also called "overseers," which signifies that they supervise and manage the church. Peter uses the verb form of *overseer* when he exhorts the elders: "Therefore, I exhort the elders among you . . . shepherd the flock of God among you, exercising oversight" (1 Peter 5:1-2). In this instance, Peter combines the concepts of shepherding and overseeing when he exhorts the elders to do their duty. Hence we can speak of the elders' overall function as being the pastoral oversight of the local church.

Helping to Meet the Flock's Many Practical Needs: In addition to the familiar, broad categories of protecting, feeding, and leading the flock, elders are also to bear responsibility for meeting the practical, diverse needs of the flock. For example, James instructs sick members of the flock to call for the elders of the church: "Is anyone among you sick? Let him call for the elders of the church, and let them pray over him, anointing him with oil in the name of the Lord" (James 5:14). Paul exhorts the Ephesian elders to care for the weak and needy of the flock: "In everything I showed you that by working hard in this manner *you must help the weak* and remember the words of the Lord Jesus, that He Himself said, 'It is more blessed to give than to receive'" (Acts 20:35; italics added).

As shepherds of the flock, the elders must be available to meet the sheep's needs. This responsibility includes: visiting the sick and comforting the bereaved; strengthening the weak; praying for *all* the sheep; visiting new members; providing counsel for couples who are engaged, married, and/or divorcing; and managing the many, day-to-day details related to the inner life of the congregation.

Hard Work and Sacrifice: When the church eldership is viewed as a status or board position in the church, there will be plenty of volunteers. When it is viewed as a demanding, pastoral work, few people will rush to volunteer. One reason there are so few shepherd elders or good church elderships is that, generally speaking, men are spiritually lazy. That is a major reason why most churches never establish a biblical eldership. Men are more than willing to let someone else fulfill their spiritual responsibilities, whether it be their wives, the clergy, or church professionals.

Biblical eldership, however, can't exist in an atmosphere of nominal Christianity. There can be no biblical eldership in a church where there is no biblical Christianity. If a biblical eldership is to function effectively, it requires men who are firmly committed to living out our Lord's principles of discipleship. Biblical eldership is dependent on men who seek first the kingdom of God and His righteousness (Matt. 6:33), men who have presented themselves as living and holy sacrifices to God and view themselves as slaves of the Lord Jesus Christ (Rom. 12:1, 2), men who love Jesus Christ above all else, men who willingly sacrifice self for the sake of others, men who seek to love as Christ loved, men who are self-disciplined and self-sacrificing, and men who have taken up the cross and are willing to suffer for Christ.

Some people say, "You can't expect laymen to rear their families, work all day, and shepherd a local church." That statement is simply not true. Many people rear families, work, and give substantial hours of time to community service, clubs, athletic activities, and/or religious institutions. The cults have built up large lay movements that survive primarily because of the volunteer time and efforts of their members. We Bible-believing Christians are becoming a lazy, soft, pay-for-it-to-be-done group of Christians. It is positively amazing how much people can accomplish when they are motivated to work toward a goal they love. I've seen people build and remodel houses in their spare time, for example. I've also seen men discipline themselves to gain a phenomenal knowledge of the Scriptures.

The real problem, then, lies not in men's limited time and energy but in false ideas about work, Christian living, life's priorities, and—especially—Christian ministry. To the Ephesian elders, Paul says, "You yourselves know that these hands ministered to my own needs and to the men who were with me. In everything I showed you that by working hard in this manner you must help the weak and remember the words of the Lord Jesus, that He Himself said, 'It is more blessed to give than to receive'" (Acts 20:34, 35). How do working men shepherd the church and still maintain a godly family life and employment? They do it by self-sacrifice, self-discipline, faith, perseverance, hard work, and the power of the Holy Spirit. R. Paul Stevens, author and instructor at Regent College in Vancouver, British Columbia, sets us on the right track when he writes:

> And for tentmakers to survive three full-time jobs (work, family and ministry), they must also adopt a sacrificial lifestyle. Tentmakers must live a pruned life and literally find leisure and rest in the rhythm of serving Christ (Matt. 11:28). They must be willing to forego a measure of career achievement and private leisure for the privilege of gaining the prize (Phil. 3:14). Many would like to be tentmakers if they could be wealthy and live a leisurely and cultured lifestyle. But the truth is that a significant ministry in the church and the community can only come by sacrifice.[5]

Shared Leadership

Shared leadership should not be a new concept to a Bible-reading Christian. Shared leadership is rooted in the Old Testament institution of the elders of Israel and in Jesus' founding of the apostolate. It is a highly significant but often overlooked fact that our Lord did not appoint one man to lead His church. He personally appointed and trained twelve men. *Jesus Christ gave the church plurality of leadership.* The Twelve comprised the first leadership council of the church and, in the most exemplary way, jointly led and taught the first Christian community. The Twelve provide a marvelous example of unity, humble brotherly love, and shared leadership structure.

Shared leadership is also evidenced by the Seven who were appointed to relieve the Twelve of the responsibility of dispensing funds to the church's widows (Acts 6:3-6). There is no indication that one of the Seven was the chief and the others were his assistants. As a body of servants, they worked on behalf of the church in Jerusalem. Based on all the evidence we have, the Seven—like the elders—formed a collective leadership council.

The New Testament reveals that the pastoral oversight of many of the first churches was committed to a plurality of elders. This was true of the earliest, Jewish-Christian churches in Jerusalem, Judea, and neighboring countries as well as many of the first Gentile churches. Interestingly enough, Protestants don't challenge the plurality of deacons in an effort to create a singular deacon, yet many challenge the plurality of elders. It is odd that most Christians have no problem accepting a plurality of deacons but are almost irrationally frightened by a plurality of elders that is far more evident in the New Testament. Despite such fears, a plurality of leadership through a council of elders needs to be preserved just as much as a plurality of deacons.

I am convinced that the underlying reason many Christians fear the plurality of elders is that they don't really understand the New Testament concept of plural elders or its rich benefits to the local church. New Testament eldership is not, as many think, a high-status, church-board position that is open to any and all who desire membership. On the contrary, an eldership patterned after the New Testament model requires qualified elder candidates to meet specific moral and spiritual qualifications before they serve (1 Tim. 3:1-7). The qualifications of such elder candidates must be publicly examined by the church (1 Tim. 3:10). The elders selected must be publicly installed into office (1 Tim. 5:22; Acts 14:23). They must be motivated and empowered by the Holy Spirit to do their work (Acts 20:28). Finally, they must be acknowledged, loved, and honored by the entire congregation. This honor given by the congregation includes the provision of financial support to elders who are uniquely gifted at preaching and teaching, which allows some elders to serve the church full or part time (1 Tim. 5:17, 18).

Thus a team of qualified, dedicated, Spirit-placed elders is not a passive, ineffective committee; it is an effective form of leadership structure that greatly benefits the church family.

A Council of Equals: Leadership by a council of elders is a form of government found in nearly every society of the ancient Near East. It was the fundamental, governmental structure of the nation of Israel throughout its Old Testament history (Ex. 3:16; Ezra 10:8). For Israel—a tribal, patriarchal society—the eldership was as basic as the family unit. So when the New Testament records that Paul, a Jew who was thoroughly immersed in the Old Testament and Jewish culture, appointed elders for his newly founded churches (Acts 14:23), it means that he established a council of elders in each local church.

By definition, the elder structure of government is a collective leadership in which each elder shares equally the position, authority, and responsibility of the office. There are different names for this type of leadership structure. More formally it is called collective, corporate, or collegiate leadership. In contemporary terms, it is referred to as multiple church leadership, plurality, shared leadership, or team leadership. I use these terms synonymously throughout this booklet. The opposite of collective leadership is unitary leadership, monarchical rule, or one-man leadership.

First Among a Council of Equals—Leaders Among Leaders: An extremely important but terribly misunderstood aspect of biblical eldership is the principle of "first among equals" (1 Tim. 5:17). Failure to understand this principle has caused some elderships to be tragically ineffective in their pastoral care and leadership. Although elders are to act jointly as a council and share equal authority and responsibility for the leadership of the church, all elders are not equal in their giftedness, biblical knowledge, leadership ability, experience, or dedication.

Therefore, those among the elders who are particularly gifted leaders and/or teachers will naturally stand out among the other elders as leaders and teachers within the leadership body. This is what the Romans called *primus inter pares*, which means "first among equals," or *primi inter pares*, which means "first ones among equals."

The principle of "first among equals" is observed first in our Lord's dealings with the twelve apostles. Jesus chose and empowered all of them to preach and heal, but He singled out three for special attention—Peter, James, and John ("first ones among equals"). Among the three, as well as among the Twelve, Peter stood out as the most prominent ("first among equals").

As the natural leader, the chief speaker, and the man of action, Peter challenged, energized, strengthened, and ignited the group. Without Peter, the group would have been less effective. When surrounded by eleven other apostles who were his equals, Peter became stronger, more balanced, and was protected from his impetuous nature and his fears. In spite of his outstanding leadership and speaking abilities, *Peter possessed no legal or official rank or title above the other eleven. They were not his subordinates. They were not his staff or team of assistants. He wasn't the apostles' "senior pastor."* He was simply first among his equals, by our Lord's approval.

The "first-among-equals" leadership relationship can also be observed among the Seven who, as we've seen, were chosen to relieve the apostles of certain responsibilities (Acts 6). Philip and Stephen stand out as prominent figures among the five other brothers (Acts 6:8-7:60; 8:5-40; 21:8). Yet, as far as the account records, the two held no special title or status above the others.

The concept of "first among equals" is further evidenced by the relationship of Paul and Barnabas during their first missionary journey. They were both apostles, yet Paul was "first among equals" because he was "the chief speaker" and dynamic leader (Acts 13:13; 14:12). Although clearly the more gifted of the two apostles, Paul held no formal ranking over Barnabas; they labored as partners in the work of the gospel. A similar relationship seems to have existed between Paul and Silas, who was also an apostle (1 Thess. 2:6).

Finally, the "first among equals" concept is evidenced by the way in which congregations are to honor their elders. Concerning elders within the church in Ephesus, Paul writes, "Let the elders who rule well be considered worthy of double honor, especially those who work hard at preaching and teaching. For the Scripture says, 'You shall not muzzle the ox while he is threshing,' and 'The laborer is worthy of his wages'" (1 Tim. 5:17, 18). All elders must be able to teach the Word, but not all of them desire to work fully at preaching and teaching. The local church should properly care for those who are specially gifted in teaching and spend the time to do so. Let us be clear about the fact that it is the spiritual giftedness of the elders that causes the church to grow and prosper spiritually, not just the eldership form of government per se.

This doesn't mean, however, that elders who are first among their equals do all the thinking and decision making for the group, or that they become the "pastors" while the others are "merely elders." To call one elder "pastor" and the rest "elders," or one elder "the clergyman" and the rest "lay elders," is to act without biblical precedence. To do so will not result in a biblical eldership. It will, at least in practice, *create a separate, superior office over the eldership, just as was done during the early second century when the division between "the overseer" and "elders" occurred.*

The advantage of the principle of "first among equals" is that *it allows for functional, gift-based diversity within the eldership team without creating an official, superior office over fellow elders.* Just as the leading apostles, such as Peter and John, bore no special title or formal distinctions from the other apostles, elders who receive double honor form no official class or receive no special title. The elders, then, who labor in the Word and exercise good leadership are, in the words of Scripture, "leading men among the brethren" (Acts 15:22).

Male Leadership

There is much about biblical eldership that offends churchgoing people today: the concept of elders who provide pastoral care, a plurality of pastors, and the idea of so-called "lay" or nonclerical pastor elders. Yet nothing is more objectionable in the minds of many contemporary people than the biblical concept of an all-male eldership. A biblical eldership, however, must be an all-male eldership.

For the Bible-believing Christian, the primary example of male leadership is found in the person of Jesus Christ. The most obvious point is that Christ came into the world as the Son of God, not the daughter of God. His maleness was not an arbitrary matter. It was a theological necessity, absolutely essential to His person and work.

During His earthly ministry, Jesus trained and appointed twelve men whom He called "apostles" (Luke 6:13). Jesus' choice of an all-male apostolate affirmed the creation order as presented in Genesis 2:18-25. Luke informs us that before choosing the Twelve Jesus spent the entire night in prayer with His Father (Luke 6:12). As the perfect Son, in complete obedience and submission to His Father's will, Jesus chose twelve males to be His apostles. These men were God the Father's choice. Jesus' choice of male apostles was based on divine principles and guidance, not local custom or traditions.

As we've seen, the Twelve followed the example of their Lord and Master by appointing seven men, not seven men and women, when they needed to establish an official body of servants to care for the church's widows and funds (Acts 6:1-6). Thirty years after Christ's ascension into heaven, Peter wrote to the churches of northwestern Asia Minor and exhorted his Christian sisters to submit to their husbands in the same way the "holy women" of the Old Testament age did (1 Peter 3:5). He also exhorted husbands to care for their wives and reminded them that their wives were fellow heirs "of the grace of life" (1 Peter 3:7). Thus Peter continued to follow His Lord's example and taught both role distinctions and male-female equality.

The biblical pattern of male leadership continued throughout the New Testament era. Regarding the marriage relationship, Paul could not have stated more pointedly the divine order of the husband-wife relationship. In complete agreement with Peter's instruction on the wife's marital submission, Paul teaches that the husband is empowered and commanded to lead in the marriage relationship and that the wife is instructed to submit "as to the Lord." The following texts speak for themselves:

- "Wives, be subject to your own husbands, as to the Lord" (Eph. 5:22).

- "But as the church is subject to Christ, so also the wives ought to be to their husbands in everything" (Eph. 5:24).

- "For the husband is the head of the wife, as Christ also is the head of the church" (Eph. 5:23).

- "Wives, be subject to your husbands, as is fitting in the Lord" (Col. 3:18).

- "But as for you, speak the things which are fitting for sound doctrine. . .that they [older women] may encourage the young women to love their husbands,

to love their children, to be sensible, pure, workers
at home, kind, being subject to their own husbands,
that the word of God may not be dishonored" (Titus
2:1, 4, 5).

Just as Paul teaches male headship in the family, he teaches
male headship in the local church (1 Tim. 2:8-3:7). Because
the family is the basic social unit and the man is the established
family authority, we should expect that men would become the
elders of the larger church family. Consider Paul's instructions
in 1 Timothy 2:12: "But I do not allow a woman to teach or
exercise authority over a man." In the same way that every
individual family is governed by certain standards of conduct,
so the local church family is governed by certain principles
of conduct and social arrangement. The letter of 1 Timothy
specifically addresses the issue of proper order and behavior
of men, women, and elders in the local church family. To his
representative in Ephesus, Paul writes, "I am writing these
things to you, hoping to come to you before long; but in case
I am delayed, *I write so that you may know how one ought to
conduct himself in the household of God,* which is the church of
the living God, the pillar and support of the truth" (1 Tim.
3:14, 15; italics added).

A major aspect of the church's social arrangement concerns
the behavior of women in the congregation. In the church in
Ephesus, as a result of false teaching that may have challenged
the validity of traditional gender roles, Christian women were
acting contrary to acceptable Christian behavior. In order to
counter improper female conduct in the church, Paul restates
Christian principles of women's conduct: "Let a woman quietly
receive instruction with entire submissiveness. But I do not
allow a woman to teach or exercise authority over a man, but to
remain quiet. For it was Adam who was first created, and then

Eve. And it was not Adam who was deceived, but the woman being quite deceived, fell into transgression" (1 Tim. 2:11-14).

First Timothy 2:11-14 should settle the question of women elders. Paul prohibits women from doing two things: (1) teaching the men of the church; and (2) exercising authority over the men.

Note that immediately following his instruction in 1 Timothy 2:11-15, that prohibits women from teaching and leading men, Paul describes the qualifications for those who oversee the local church (1 Tim. 3:1-7). Significantly, the qualifications assume a male subject. Thus the overseer is to be "the husband of one wife" and "one who manages his own household well" (1 Tim. 3:2, 4). Paul gives no suggestion of women elders in this passage.

Qualified Leadership

In a letter to a young presbyter named Nepotian, dated A.D. 394, Jerome (A.D. 345-419) rebukes the churches of his day for their hypocrisy in showing more concern for the appearance of their church buildings than the careful selection of their church leaders: "Many build churches nowadays; their walls and pillars of glowing marble, their ceilings glittering with gold, their altars studded with jewels. Yet to the choice of Christ's ministers no heed is paid."[6]

Multitudes of churches today repeat similar error. Many of them seem oblivious to the biblical requirements for their spiritual leaders as well as to the need for each congregation to properly examine all candidates for leadership qualities in light of biblical standards (1 Tim. 3:10). The most common mistake made by churches that are eager to implement biblical eldership is to appoint biblically unqualified men. Because there is always a need for more shepherds, it is tempting to allow unqualified, unprepared men to assume leadership in the church. This is, however, a time-proven formula for failure. A biblical eldership requires biblically qualified elders.

The overriding concern of the New Testament in relation to church leadership is to ensure that the right kind of men will serve as elders and deacons. The offices of God's church are not honorary positions bestowed on individuals who have attended church faithfully or who are senior in years. Nor are these offices to be viewed as church-board positions to be filled with good friends, rich donors, or charismatic personalities. Nor are they positions that only graduate seminary students can fill. The church offices—both eldership and deaconship—are open to all men who meet the apostolic, biblical requirements. The New Testament unequivocally emphasizes this. Consider these points:

- To the troubled church in Ephesus, Paul insists that a properly constituted, biblical Christian church (1 Tim. 3:14, 15) must have qualified, approved elders:

  It is a trustworthy statement: if any man aspires to the office of overseer, it is a fine work he desires to do. *An overseer, then, must be* above reproach, the husband of one wife, temperate, prudent, respectable, hospitable, able to teach, not addicted to wine or pugnacious, but gentle, uncontentious, free from the love of money. *He must be* one who manages his own household well, keeping his children under control with all dignity (but if a man does not know how to manage his own household, how will he take care of the church of God?); and not a new convert, lest he become conceited and fall into the condemnation incurred by the devil. And *he must have* a good reputation with those outside the church, so that he may not fall into reproach and the snare of the devil (1 Tim. 3:1-7; italics added).

- Paul, as we've seen, also insists that prospective elders and deacons be publicly examined in light of the stated list of qualifications. He writes, "And let these [deacons] also [like the elders] first be tested [examined]; then let them serve as deacons if they are beyond reproach" (1 Tim 3:10; cf. 5:24, 25).

- When directing Titus in how to organize churches on the island of Crete, Paul reminds him to appoint only morally and spiritually qualified men to be elders. By stating elder qualifications in a letter, Paul establishes a public list that will guide the local church in its choice of elders and empower it to hold its elders accountable:

  > For this reason I left you in Crete, that you might set in order what remains, and appoint elders in every city *as I directed you, namely, if any man be* above reproach, the husband of one wife, having children who believe, not accused of dissipation or rebellion. For the *overseer must be* above reproach as God's steward, not self-willed, not quick-tempered, not addicted to wine, not pugnacious, not fond of sordid gain, but hospitable, loving what is good, sensible, just, devout, self-controlled, holding fast the faithful word which is in accordance with the teaching, that he may be able both to exhort in sound doctrine and to refute those who contradict (Titus 1:5-9; italics added).

- When writing to churches scattered throughout northwestern Asia Minor, Peter speaks of the kind of men who should be elders. He exhorts the elders to shepherd the flock "not under compulsion, but voluntarily, according to the will of God; and not for sordid gain, but with eagerness; nor yet as lording it over those allotted to your charge, but proving to be examples to the flock" (1 Peter 5:2, 3).

It is highly noteworthy that the New Testament provides more instruction concerning the qualifications for eldership than on any other aspect of eldership. Such qualifications are not required of all teachers or evangelists. One person may be gifted as an evangelist and be used of God in that capacity, yet be unqualified to be an elder. An individual may be an evangelist immediately after conversion, but Scripture says that a new convert cannot be an elder (1 Tim. 3:6).

When we speak of the elders' qualifications, most people think that these qualifications are different than those of the clergy. The New Testament, however, has no separate standards for professional clergy and lay elders. The reason is simple. There aren't three separate offices—pastor, elders, and deacons—in the New Testament-style local church. There are only two offices—elders and deacons. From the New Testament perspective, any man in the congregation who desires to shepherd the Lord's people and meets God's requirements for the office can be a pastor elder.

The scriptural qualifications can be divided into three broad categories relating to moral and spiritual character, abilities, and Spirit-given motivation.

Moral and Spiritual Character: Most of the biblical qualifications relate to each candidate's moral and spiritual qualities. The first, overarching qualification is that of being "above reproach." The meaning of "above reproach" is defined by the character qualities that follow the term. In both of Paul's lists of elder qualifications, the first, specific, character virtue itemized is "the husband of one wife." This means that each elder must be above reproach in his marital and sexual life.

The other character qualities stress the elder's integrity, self-control, and spiritual maturity. Since elders govern the church body, each one must be self-controlled in the use of money, alcohol, and the exercise of his pastoral authority. Since each elder is to be a model of Christian living, he must be spiritually devout, righteous, a lover of good, hospitable, and morally above reproach before the non-Christian community. In pastoral work, relationship skills are preeminent. Thus a shepherd elder must be gentle, stable, sound-minded, and uncontentious. An angry, hotheaded man hurts people. So, an elder must not have a dictatorial spirit or be quick-tempered, pugnacious, or self-willed. Finally, an elder must not be a new Christian. He must be a spiritually mature, humble, time-proven disciple of Jesus Christ.

Abilities: Within the lists of elder qualifications, three requirements address the elder's abilities to perform the task. He must be able to manage his family household well, provide a model of Christian living for others to follow, and be able to teach and defend the faith.

Able to manage his family household well: An elder must be able to manage his family household well. The Scripture states, "He must be one who manages his own household well, keeping his children under control with all dignity (but if a man does not know how to manage his own household, how will he take care of the church of God?)" (1 Tim. 3:4, 5). The Puritans referred to the family household as the "little church." This perspective is in keeping with the scriptural reasoning that if a man cannot shepherd his family, he can't shepherd the extended family of the church. Managing the local church is more like managing a family than managing a business or state. A man may be a successful businessman, a capable public official, a brilliant office manager, or a top military leader but be a terrible church elder or father. Thus a man's ability to oversee his family household well is a prerequisite for overseeing God's household.

Able to provide a model for others to follow: An elder must be an example of Christian living that others will want to follow. Peter reminds the Asian elders "to be examples to the flock" (1 Peter 5:3). If a man is not a godly model for others to follow, he cannot be an elder even if he is a good teacher and manager. The greatest way to inspire and influence people for God is through personal example. Character and deeds, not official position or title, are what really influence people for eternity. Today men and women crave authentic examples of true Christianity in action. Who can better provide the week-by-week, long-term examples of family life, business life, and church life than a local-church elder? That is why it is so important that an elder, as a living imitator of Christ, shepherd God's flock in God's way.

Able to teach and defend the faith: An elder must be able to teach and defend the faith. It doesn't matter how successful a man is in his business, how eloquently he speaks, or how intelligent he is. If he isn't firmly committed to historic, apostolic doctrine and able to instruct people in biblical doctrine, he does not qualify to be a biblical elder (1 Tim. 3:2; Titus 1:9).

The New Testament requires that a pastor elder "[hold] fast the faithful word which is in accordance with the teaching" (Titus 1:9). This means that an elder must firmly adhere to orthodox, historic, biblical teaching. "Elders must not," one commentator says, "be chosen from among those who have been toying with new doctrines."[7] Since the local church is "the pillar and support of the truth" (1 Tim. 3:15), its leaders must be rock-solid pillars of biblical doctrine or the house will crumble. Since the local church is also a small flock traveling over treacherous terrain that is infested with "savage wolves," only those shepherds who know the way and see the wolves can lead the flock safely to its destination. An elder, then, must be characterized by doctrinal integrity.

It is essential for an elder to be firmly committed to apostolic, biblical doctrine so "that he may be able both to exhort in sound doctrine and to refute those who contradict" (Titus 1:9). This requires that a prospective elder must have applied himself for some years to the reading and study of Scripture, that he can reason intelligently and logically discuss biblical issues, that he has formulated doctrinal beliefs, and that he has the verbal ability and willingness to teach other people. There should be no confusion, then, about what a New Testament elder is called to do. He is to teach and exhort the congregation in sound doctrine and to defend the truth from false teachers. This is the big difference between board elders and pastor elders. New Testament elders are both guardians and teachers of sound, biblical doctrine.

Spirit-given Motivation for the Task: An obvious but not insignificant qualification is the elder's personal desire to love and care for God's people. Paul and the first Christians applaud such willingness and created this popular Christian saying: "If any man aspires to the office of overseer, it is a fine work he desires to do" (1 Tim. 3:1). Peter, too, insists that an elder must shepherd the flock willingly and voluntarily (1 Peter 5:2). He knew from years of personal experience that someone who views spiritual care as an unwanted obligation cannot fulfill the shepherding task. An elder who serves grudgingly or under constraint is incapable of genuinely caring for people. He will be an unhappy, impatient, guilty, fearful, and ineffective shepherd. Shepherding God's people through this sin-weary world is far too difficult a task—fraught with too many problems, dangers, and demands—to be entrusted to someone who lacks the will and desire to do the work effectively.

A true desire to lead the family of God is always a Spirit-generated desire. Paul reminds the Ephesian elders that the

Holy Spirit—not the church or the apostles—placed them as overseers in the church to shepherd the flock of God (Acts 20:28). The Spirit called them to shepherd the church and moved them to care for the flock. The Spirit planted the pastoral desire in their hearts. He gave them the compulsion and strength to do the work and also the wisdom and appropriate gifts to care for the flock. The elders were His wise choice to complete the task. In the church of God, it is not man's will that matters; it is God's will and arrangement that matter. So, the only men who qualify for eldership are those whom the Holy Spirit gives the motivation and gifts for the task.

A biblical eldership, then, is a biblically qualified team of shepherd leaders. A plurality of unqualified elders provides no significant benefit to the local church. I agree fully with the counsel of Jon Zens, who writes, "Better have no elders than the wrong ones."[8] The local church must in all earnestness insist on biblically qualified elders, even if such men take years to develop.

Servant Leadership

Just as Christianity influenced the Roman Empire, the Greco-Roman world also affected the course of Christianity. Citing pagan influences on early Christianity, Kenneth Scott Latourette—renowned church historian and professor of Christian missions—states that the Roman concepts of power and rule corrupted the organization and life of early churches. He observes that "the Church was being interpenetrated by ideals which were quite contrary to the Gospel, especially the conception and use of power which were in stark contrast to the kind exhibited in the life and teaching of Jesus and in the cross and the resurrection."[9] This, Latourette goes on to say, proved to be "the menace which was most nearly disastrous" to Christianity.[10]

I believe it is more accurate to say that the conceptual and structural changes that occurred within the church during the early centuries of Christianity proved to be disastrous. Christianity, the humblest of all faiths, degenerated into the most power-hungry and hierarchical religion on earth. After Emperor Constantine elevated Christianity to legal religious status in A.D. 312, the once-persecuted Christians fiercely persecuted all their opposition. An unscriptural clerical and priestly caste arose that was consumed by the quest for power, position, and authority. Even Roman emperors had a guiding hand in the development of Christian churches. The pristine character of the New Testament church community was lost.

When we read the Gospels, however, we see that the principles of brotherly community, love, humility, and servanthood are at the very heart of Christ's teaching. Unfortunately, like many of the early Christians, we have been slow to understand these great virtues and especially slow to apply them to church structure and leadership style.

New Testament, Christlike elders are to be servant leaders, not rulers or dictators. God doesn't want His people to be used by petty, self-serving tyrants. Elders are to choose a life of service on behalf of others. Like the servant Christ, they are to sacrifice their time and energy for the good of others. Only elders who are loving, humble servants can genuinely manifest the incomparable life of Jesus Christ to their congregations and a watching world.

A group of elders, however, can become a self-serving, autocratic leadership body. Thus Peter, using the same terminology as Jesus, warns the Asian elders against abusive, lordly leadership: ". . . nor yet as lording it over those allotted to your charge, but proving to be examples to the flock" (1 Peter 5:3). Peter also charges the elders, as well as everyone else in the congregation, to clothe themselves in humility just as Jesus clothed Himself in humility: "All of you, clothe yourselves with humility toward one another, for God is opposed to the proud, but gives grace to the humble" (1 Peter 5:5). With similar concern, Paul reminds the Ephesian elders of his example of humility. In Acts 20:19, he describes his manner of "serving the Lord with all humility" and implies that they, too, must serve the Lord in the same manner. Because of pride's lurking temptation, a new Christian should not be an elder: "And not a new convert, lest he become conceited and fall into the condemnation incurred by the devil" (1 Tim. 3:6).

In addition to shepherding others with a servant spirit, the elders must humbly and lovingly relate to one another. They must be able to patiently build consensus, compromise, persuade, listen, handle disagreement, forgive, receive rebuke and correction, confess sin, and appreciate the wisdom and perspective of others—even those with whom they disagree. They must be able to submit to one another, speak kindly and gently to one another, be patient with their fellow colleagues, defer to one another, and speak their minds openly in truth and love. Stronger and more gifted elders must not use their giftedness, as talented people sometimes do, to force their own way by threatening to leave the church and take their followers with them. Such selfishness creates ugly, carnal power struggles that endanger the unity and peace of the entire congregation.

The humble-servant character of the eldership doesn't imply, however, an absence of authority. The New Testament terms that describe the elders' position and work—"God's stewards," "overseers," "shepherd," "leading"—imply authority as well as responsibility. Peter could not have warned the Asian elders against "lording it over those allotted to your charge" (1 Peter 5:3) if they had no authority. As shepherds of the church, elders have been given the authority to lead and protect the local church (Acts 20:28-31). The key issue is the attitude in which elders exercise that authority.

Following the biblical model, elders must not wield the authority given to them in a heavy-handed way. They must not use manipulative tactics, play power games, or be arrogant and aloof. They must never think that they are unanswerable to their fellow brethren or to God. Elders must not be authoritarian, which is incompatible with humble servanthood. When we consider Paul's example and that of our Lord's, we must agree that biblical elders do not dictate; they direct. True elders do not command the consciences of their brethren but appeal to their brethren to faithfully follow God's Word. Out of love, true elders suffer and bear the brunt of difficult people and problems so that the lambs are not bruised. The elders bear the misunderstandings and sins of other people so that the assembly may live in peace. They lose sleep so that others may rest. They make great personal sacrifices of time and energy for the welfare of others. They see themselves as men under authority. They depend on God for wisdom and help, not on their own power and cleverness. They face the false teachers' fierce attacks. They guard the community's liberty and freedom in Christ so that the saints are encouraged to develop their gifts, to mature, and to serve one another.

In summary, using Paul's great love chapter, we can say that a servant elder "is patient . . . kind . . . not jealous; . . . [a servant elder] does not brag . . . [a servant elder] is not arrogant, does not act unbecomingly . . . does not seek [his] . . . own . . . [a servant elder] is not provoked, does not take into account a wrong suffered, does not rejoice in unrighteousness, but rejoices with the truth; [a servant elder] bears all things, believes all things, hopes all things, endures all things" (1 Cor. 13:4-7).

Biblical Evidence
for Pastoral Leadership
by the Plurality of Elders

———

Christians who profess the Bible to be God's infallible, all-sufficient Word agree that they must establish their church practices and doctrines on the teachings of the Bible. Many contemporary scholars say, however, that the New Testament is ambiguous or silent regarding the topic of church government and conclude that no one can insist upon a biblical model of church government (by elders or anyone else) for all churches because the Bible doesn't. George Eldon Ladd, author of *A Theology of the New Testament* and former professor at Fuller Theological Seminary, expresses this view most concisely: "It appears likely that there was no normative pattern of church government in the apostolic age, and that the organizational structure of the church is no essential element in the theology of the church."[11] Although this is a widely held view among scholars today, it must be challenged because it simply does not fit biblical evidence.

In its major features, local church leadership (or government) by the plurality of elders is plainly and amply set forth by the New Testament writers. J. Alec Motyer, former principal of Trinity College in Bristol, England, captures the true spirit of the New Testament when he writes, ". . . it is not as much as hinted in the New Testament that the church would ever need—or indeed should ever want or tolerate—any other local leadership than that of the eldership group."[12]

Not only does the New Testament record the existence of elders in numerous churches, it also gives instruction about elders and to elders. In fact, the New Testament offers more instruction regarding elders than it does regarding such important church subjects such as the Lord's Supper, the Lord's Day, baptism, and spiritual gifts. When you consider the New Testament's characteristic avoidance of detailed regulation and church procedures (when it is compared to the Old Testament), the attention given to elders is amazing. "This is why," writes Jon Zens, editor of the journal *Searching Together*, "we need to seriously consider the doctrine of eldership; it jumps out at us from the pages of the New Testament, yet it has fallen into disrepute and is not being practiced as a whole in local churches."[13]

A Consistent, New Testament Pattern

To hear some scholars speak, you would think that the Bible doesn't say one word about church elders or church government. But that is not true. The New Testament records evidence of pastoral oversight by a council of elders in nearly all the first churches. These local churches were spread over a wide geographical and culturally diverse area—from Jerusalem to Rome.

Examples of Eldership: Consider, as recorded in the New Testament, the consistent pattern of plural leadership by elders that existed among the first Christian churches.

- Elders are found in the churches of Judea and the surrounding area (Acts 11:30; James 5:14, 15).

- Elders governed the church in Jerusalem (Acts 15, 21).

- Among the Pauline churches, leadership by the plurality of elders was established in the churches in

Derbe, Lystra, Iconium, and Antioch (Acts 14:20-23); in the church in Ephesus (Acts 20:17; 1 Tim. 3:1-7; 5:17-25); in the church in Philippi (Phil. 1:1); and in the churches on the island of Crete (Titus 1:5).

■ According to the well-traveled letter of 1 Peter, elders existed in churches throughout northwestern Asia Minor: Pontus, Galatia, Cappadocia, Asia, and Bithynia (1 Peter 1:1; 5:1).

■ There are strong indications that elders existed in churches in Thessalonica (1 Thess. 5:12) and Rome (Heb. 13:17).

Instruction About Elders: Not only does the New Testament provide examples of elder-led churches, it includes explicit instructions to churches about how to care for, protect, discipline, select, restore, and call the elders. The apostles intended these instructions to be obeyed, and they should be regarded as normative teaching for all Christian churches at all times.

■ James instructs those who are sick to call for the elders of the church (James 5:14).

■ Paul instructs the Ephesian church to financially support elders who labor "at preaching and teaching" (1 Tim. 5:17, 18).

■ Paul instructs the local church about protecting elders from false accusation, disciplining elders who sin, and restoring fallen elders (1 Tim. 5:19-22).

■ Paul instructs the church regarding the proper qualifications for eldership (1 Tim. 3:1-7; Titus 1:5-9).

- To the church in Ephesus, Paul states that anyone who desires to be an elder desires a "fine work" (1 Tim. 3:1).

- Paul instructs the church to examine the qualifications of prospective elders (1 Tim. 3:10; 5:24, 25).

- Peter instructs the young men of the church to submit to church elders (1 Peter 5:5).

- Paul teaches that elders are the household stewards, leaders, instructors, and teachers of the local church (1 Thess. 5:12; Titus 1:7, 9).

Instruction and Exhortation to Elders: Besides giving instruction to churches about elders, Paul, Peter, and James give these instructions directly to elders:

- James tells elders to pray for the sick and anoint them with oil in the name of the Lord Jesus (James 5:14).

- Peter directly charges elders to willingly pastor and oversee the local congregation (1 Peter 5:1, 2).

- Peter warns elders not to be domineering (1 Peter 5:3).

- Peter promises elders that when the Lord Jesus returns they will receive "the unfading crown of glory" (1 Peter 5:4)

- Peter exhorts elders to be clothed in humility (1 Peter 5:5).

- Paul reminds the Ephesian elders that the Holy Spirit placed them in the church to be overseers and pastor the church of God (Acts 20:28).

- Paul exhorts elders to guard the church from false

teachers (Acts 20:28) and to be alert to the constant threat of false doctrine. (Acts 20:31).

■ Paul reminds elders to work hard, help the needy, and be generous like the Lord Jesus Christ (Acts 20:35).

Promotes the True Nature of the New Testament-Style Local Church

The local church's structure of government makes a profound statement about the nature of the local church and its philosophy of ministry. The local church is not an undefined mass of people; it is a particular group of people that has a unique character, mission, and purpose. I am convinced that the elder structure of government best harmonizes with and promotes the true nature of the local church as revealed in the New Testament. We will consider four ways in which the elder structure of government complements the nature and theology of the local church.

The Church Is a Close-knit Family of Brothers and Sisters: Of the different New Testament terms used to describe the nature of the church—the body, the bride, the temple, the flock—the one most frequently used is the family, particularly the fraternal aspect of the family—brothers and sisters. Robert Banks, a prominent leader in the worldwide, home-church movement, makes this observation in his book, *Paul's Idea of Community*:

> Although in recent years Paul's metaphors for community have been subjected to quite intense study, especially his description of it as a "body," his application to it of "household" or "family" terminology has all too often been overlooked or only mentioned in passing.[14]

Banks further comments on the frequency and significance of these familial expressions:

> So numerous are these, and so frequently do they appear, that the comparison of the Christian community with a "family" must be regarded as the most significant metaphorical usage of all. . . . More than any of the other images utilized by Paul, it reveals the essence of his thinking about community.[15]

The local Christian church, then, is to be a close-knit family of brothers and sisters. Brotherliness also provided a key guiding principle for the management of relationships between Christians (Rom. 14:15, 21; 1 Cor. 6:8; 8:11-13; 2 Thess. 3:14, 15; Philem. 15, 16; James 4:11). Jesus insisted that His followers were true brothers and sisters and that none among them should act like the rabbis of His day who elevated themselves above their fellow countrymen:

> "But they do all their deeds to be noticed by men; for they broaden their phylacteries, and lengthen the tassels of their garments. And they love the place of honor at banquets, and the chief seats in the synagogues, and respectful greetings in the market places, and being called by men, Rabbi. *But do not be called Rabbi*; for One is your Teacher, and *you are all brothers*" (Matt. 23:5-8; italics added).

In complete obedience to Christ's teaching on humility and brotherhood, the first Christians resisted special titles, sacred clothing, chief seats, and lordly terminology to highlight their community leaders. They also chose an appropriate leadership structure for their local congregations—leadership by a council of elders. The first Christians found within their biblical heritage a structure of government that was compatible with their new, spiritual family and their theological beliefs. Israel was a great family, composed of many individual families. The nation found leadership by a plurality of elders to be a suitable form of self-government that provided fair representation to its members. The same is true of the local Christian church. The elder structure of government suits an extended family organization like the local church. It allows any brother in the community who desires it and qualifies for it to share fully in the leadership of the community.

The Church Is a Nonclerical Community: The local church is not only an intimate, loving family of redeemed brothers and sisters, it is a nonclerical family. Unlike Israel, which was divided into sacred priestly members and lay members, the first-century, Christian church was a people's movement. The distinguishing mark of Christianity was not found in a clerical hierarchy but in the fact that God's Spirit came to dwell within ordinary, common people and that through them the Spirit manifested Jesus' life to the believing community and the world.

It is an immensely profound truth that no special priestly or clerical class that is distinct from the whole people of God appears in the New Testament. Under the new covenant ratified by the blood of Christ, every member of the church of Jesus Christ is a holy saint, a royal priest, and a Spirit-gifted member of the body of Christ. Paul teaches that a wide diversity of gifts and services exists within the body of Christ (1 Cor. 12), but he says nothing about a mystical gap between sacred clergy and common laity. If it exists, surely something as fundamental to the Church as a clergy-laity division should at least be mentioned in the New Testament. The New Testament, however, stresses the oneness of the people of God (Eph. 2:13-19) and the dismantling of the sacred-secular concept that existed between priests and people under the old covenant (1 Peter 2:5-10; Rev. 1:6).

Clericalism does not represent biblical, apostolic Christianity. Indeed, the real error to be contended with is not simply that one man provides leadership for the congregation, but that one person in the holy brotherhood has been sacralized apart from the brotherhood to an unscriptural status. In practice, the ordained clergyman—the minister, the reverend—is *the Protestant priest.*

Biblical eldership cannot exist in an environment of clericalism. Paul's employment of the elder structure of government for the local church is clear, practical evidence against clericalism because the eldership is nonclerical in nature. The elders are always viewed in the Bible as "elders of the people" or "elders of the congregation," never "elders of God." The elders represent the people as leading members from among the people.

When establishing churches, Paul never ordains a priest or cleric to perform the church's ministry. When he establishes a church, he leaves behind a council of elders chosen from among the believers to jointly oversee the local community (Acts 14:23; Titus 1:5). Obviously that was all he believed that a local church needed. Since the local congregation of his day was composed of saints, priests, and Spirit-empowered servants, and since Christ was present with each congregation through the person of the Holy Spirit, none of the traditional, religious trappings such as sacred sites, sacred buildings, or sacred personnel (priests, clerics, or holy men) were needed. Nor could such be tolerated. To meet the need for community leadership and protection, Paul provides the nonclerical, elder structure of government—a form of government that would not demean the lordship of Christ over His people or the glorious status of a priestly, saintly body of people in which every member ministered.

The Church Is a Humble-Servant Community: I am convinced that one reason the apostles chose the elder system of government was because it enhanced the loving, humble-servant character of the Christian family. The New Testament offers a consistent example of shared leadership as the ideal structure of leadership in a congregation where love, humility, and servanthood are paramount. When it functions properly, shared leadership requires a greater exercise of humble servanthood than does unitary leadership. In order for an eldership to operate effectively, the elders must show mutual regard for one another, submit themselves one to another, patiently wait upon one another, genuinely consider one another's interests and perspectives, and defer to one another. Eldership, then, enhances brotherly love, humility, mutuality, patience, and loving interdependence—qualities that are to mark the servant church.

Furthermore, shared leadership is often more trying than unitary leadership. It exposes our impatience with one another, our stubborn pride, our bullheadedness, our selfish immaturity, our domineering disposition, our lack of love and understanding of one another, and our prayerlessness. It also shows how underdeveloped and immature we really are in humility, brotherly love, and the true servant spirit. Like the saints at Corinth, we are quick to develop our knowledge and public gifts but slow to mature in love and humility.

I believe that churches today desperately need a revival of love, humility, and the servant spirit. Such a revival must begin with our leaders, and biblical eldership provides the structure through which leaders learn to work together in mutual love and humility. Since the eldership represents a microcosm of the entire church, it provides a living model of loving relationships and servanthood for the entire body. Thus, leadership by a plurality of elders ideally suits the humble-servant church.

The Church Is Under Christ's Headship: Most important, biblical eldership guards and promotes the preeminence and position of Christ over the local church. Jesus left His disciples with the precious promise that "where two or three have gathered together in My name, there I am in their midst" (Matt. 18:20). Because the apostles knew that Jesus Christ, by the Holy Spirit, was uniquely present with them as Ruler, Head, Lord, Pastor, Master, Overseer, High Priest, and King, they chose a form of government that reflected this distinctive, fundamental, Christian truth. This truth was not a theoretical idea to the early Christians—it was reality. The first churches were truly Christ-centered and Christ-dependent. Christ alone provided all they needed in order to be in full fellowship with God and one another. Christ's person and work was so infinitely great, final, and complete that nothing—even in appearance—could diminish the centrality of His presence among and sufficiency for His people.

So, during the first century no Christian would have dared to take the position or title of sole ruler, overseer, or pastor of the church. We Christians today, however, are so accustomed to speaking of "the pastor" that we do not stop to realize that the New Testament does not. This fact is profoundly significant, and we must not permit our customary practice to shield our minds from this important truth. There is only one flock and one Pastor (John 10:16), one body and one Head (Col. 1:18), one holy priesthood and one great High Priest (Heb. 4:14ff), one brotherhood and one Elder Brother (Rom. 8:29), one building and one Cornerstone (1 Peter 2:5ff), one Mediator, and one Lord. Jesus Christ is the "Senior Pastor," and all others are His undershepherds (1 Peter 5:4).

To symbolize the reality of Christ's leadership and presence over the local church and its leaders, one church places an empty chair at the table next to the chairman during all elders' meetings. This is a visual reminder to the elders of Christ's presence and lordship, of their position as His undershepherds, and of their dependence on Him through prayer and the Word.

Promotes the Protection and Sanctification of Spiritual Leaders

We come now to two extremely significant reasons for and benefits of pastoral leadership by a council of qualified elders. First, the shared leadership structure of eldership provides necessary accountability and protection from the particular sins that plague spiritual leaders. In turn, this protects the spiritual character of the local church and the testimony of the Lord's name. Second, the eldership structure provides peer relationships to help balance elders' weaknesses and correct their character, an essential component in the sanctification process of spiritual leaders.

Leadership Accountability: English historian Lord Acton said, "Power tends to corrupt, and absolute power corrupts absolutely." Because of our biblical beliefs in the dreadful realities of sin, the curse, Satan, and human depravity, we should understand well why people in positions of power are easily corrupted. In fact, the better we understand the exceeding sinfulness and deceitfulness of sin, the stronger our commitment to accountability will be. The collective leadership of a biblical eldership provides a formal structure for genuine accountability.

Shared, brotherly leadership provides needed restraint concerning such sins as pride, greed, and "playing god." Earl D. Radmacher, chancellor of a Baptist seminary in America, writes, "Human leaders, even Christian ones, are sinners and they only accomplish God's will imperfectly. Multiple leaders, therefore, will serve as a 'check and balance' on each other and serve as a safeguard against the very human tendency to play God over other people."[16]

It was never our Lord's will for one individual to control the local church. The concept of the pastor as the lonely, trained professional—the sacred person presiding over the church who can never really become a part of the congregation—is utterly unscriptural. Not only is this concept unscriptural, it is psychologically and spiritually unhealthy. Radmacher goes on to contrast the deficiencies of a church leadership that is placed primarily in the hands of one pastor to the wholesomeness of leadership when it is shared by multiple pastors:

> Laymen . . . are indifferent because they are so busy. They have no time to bother with church matters. Church administration is left, therefore, largely in the hands of the pastor. This is bad for him, and it is bad also for the church. It makes it easier for the minister to build up in himself a dictatorial disposition and to nourish in his heart the love of autocratic power.
>
> It is my conviction that God has provided a hedge against these powerful temptations by the concept of multiple elders. The check and balance that is provided by men of equal authority is most wholesome and helps to bring about the desired attitude expressed by Peter to the plurality of elders: ". . . shepherd the flock of God among you, not under compulsion, but voluntarily, according to the will of God; and not for sordid gain, but with eagerness; nor yet as lording it over those allotted to your charge, but proving to be examples to the flock (1 Peter 5:2, 3)."[17]

In addition to providing close accountability, genuine partnership, and peer relationships—the very things most imperial pastors shrink from at all costs—shared leadership provides the local church shepherd with accountability for his work. Church leaders (like all of us) can be lazy, forgetful, fearful, or too busy to fulfill their responsibilities. Thus they need colleagues in ministry to whom they are answerable for their work. Coaches know that athletes who train together push one another to greater achievement. When someone else is running alongside him or her, a runner will push a little harder and go a little faster. The same is true in the Lord's work. That is one reason why the Lord sent out His disciples in twos.

Peer Relationships: One of the deep joys of my life has been to share the pastoral leadership of a church with a team of dedicated pastor elders. As partners in the work of shepherding God's precious, blood-bought people, we have sharpened, balanced, comforted, protected, and strengthened one another through nearly every conceivable life situation. I do not hesitate to say that the relationship with my fellow elders has been the most important tool God has used, outside of my marriage relationship, for the spiritual development of my Christian character, leadership abilities, and teaching ministry. The eldership has played a major role in the sanctification process of my Christian life.

Shared leadership can provide a church leader with critically needed recognition of his faults and deficiencies and can help to offset them. We all have blind spots, eccentricities, and deficiencies. We all have what C. S. Lewis called "a fatal flaw."[18] We can see these fatal flaws so clearly in others but not in ourselves. These fatal flaws or blind spots distort our judgment. They deceive us. They can even destroy us. This is particularly true of multitalented, charismatic leaders. Blind to their flaws and extreme views, some talented leaders have destroyed themselves because they had no peers who could confront and balance them and, in fact, wanted none.

When a single leader is atop a pyramidal structure of organization, the important balancing of one another's weaknesses and strengths normally does not occur. Note the strong language Robert Greenleaf, author of the book *Servant Leadership*, uses to convey his observations:

> To be a lone chief atop a pyramid is *abnormal and corrupting*. None of us are perfect by ourselves, and all of us need the help and correcting influence of close colleagues. When someone is moved atop a pyramid, that person no longer has colleagues, only subordinates. Even the frankest and bravest of subordinates do not talk with their boss in the same way that they talk with colleagues who are equals, and normal communication patterns become warped.[19]

I believe that traditional, single-church pastors would improve their character and ministry if they had genuine peers to whom they were regularly accountable and with whom they worked jointly.

An Apostolic Directive

———

Since Paul established the elder structure of government among Gentile churches (Acts 14:23) and, most likely, the Twelve established it among Jewish churches (Acts 15:6; James 5:14), the New Testament writers assumed eldership to be a fixed, apostolic institution. In Titus 1:5, Paul tells Titus and the churches that a church is not properly ordered until qualified elders (plural) have been appointed. So he orders Titus to install elders: "Appoint elders in every city as I directed you" (Titus 1:5*b*). By doing this, Paul is going against customary cultural practices because both the Jewish synagogue and Greco-Roman society commonly practiced one-man oversight. Thus Paul's choice of the elder structure of government is intentional. He is not simply accommodating himself to current social norms. His instruction to Titus establishes an apostolic directive that should be followed by Christians today.

Many scholars contend, however, that only the instructions about elders, not the elder structure, are universally binding on churches. They say that Paul's instructions regarding the qualifications of an elder are binding but that the structure is not. By making this distinction, they can eliminate the eldership structure from the church and apply the biblical instructions to their self-appointed institutions—the clerical structure or the singular pastorate. But this is an erroneous distinction. How, for example, would a critically important passage such as 1 Timothy 5:17, 18 apply to the singular pastorate? This instruction makes sense only in the context of a plurality of elders.

I conclude, therefore, that the instructions given to elders and about elders, as well as the eldership structure itself, are to be regarded as apostolic directives (Titus 1:5) that are normative for churches today. Ladd is quite wrong when he claims that "there was no normative pattern of church government in the apostolic age, and that the organizational structure of the church is no essential element in the theology of the church."[20]

We would do well to heed Alfred Kuen's sober warning against doubting the full sufficiency of Scripture in order to direct the practices of our churches today. Kuen, a Bible teacher at the Emmaus Bible Institute in Switzerland, writes:

> Has not the history of twenty centuries of Christianity proved that the plan of the primitive church is the only one which is suitable for all times and places, is most flexible in its adaptation to the most diverse conditions,

is the best able to resist and stand against persecutions, and offers the maximum of possibilities for the full development of the spiritual life?

Each time that man has believed himself to be more intelligent than God, that he has painstakingly developed a religious system "better adapted to the psychology of man," more conformable to the spirit of our times, instead of simply following the neotestamentary model, his attempt has been short-lived because of failure due to some unforeseen difficulty.

All heresies and deviations in the church spring from the abandonment of the Scripture and of the model for the church which they present.[21]

In short, as Alfred Kuen concludes, "the churches established by the apostles remain the valid models for churches of all times and places."[22]

Conclusion

———

A filing cabinet drawer full of objections can be raised against pastoral leadership by a plurality of elders. For the Bible-believing Christian, however, the real issue is this: is pastoral leadership by a plurality of elders biblical? Is it apostolic? It is my contention that it is! Both the apostles Paul and Peter mandate that the local church elders pastor the flock of God (Acts 20:28; 1 Peter 5:1, 2; cf. Titus 1:5). We have no right, then, to take away the elders' God-given mandate. Yet that is precisely what most churches have done by applying the apostolic mandate to shepherd the local church to a single, professional pastor and by subordinating the eldership to the pastor. Where in the New Testament do we find references to the ordained (reverend-clergyman) pastor and his advising elders? We don't! We find only pastor elders mentioned.

We must admit, however, that most traditional, clergy-led churches will find pastoral leadership by a plurality of qualified pastor elders to be difficult if not impossible to implement. So, to try to implement biblical eldership will require two conditions. First, each local church and its leaders must be firmly convinced that eldership is a scriptural teaching. Second, the local church must be committed to make the difficult, personal changes necessary in order to make eldership work for God's glory.

These two conditions, of course, are essential when implementing any unfamiliar or difficult biblical practice or doctrine. If you were to ask, for example, "does marriage work?" many people would answer that it doesn't appear to be working. So should we discard the institution of marriage and look for something better? No! The marriage institution is God's will for the human race, as revealed in the Bible. So, in order to make marriage work we must first believe it to be a biblical teaching and then be committed to making it work. Only then will marriage work. The same conditions hold true for implementing a biblical eldership. We must believe it is scriptural and be committed by God's help to making it work effectively.

To be sure, the incorporation of pastoral eldership into the local church is not the cure-all for every problem. Eldership creates its own problems, and these must be understood and continually addressed. However, when properly implemented, biblical eldership allows the church to be what God designed it to be, fosters the spiritual development of the leading men within the church family, and honors the teaching of God's precious Word.

1. Ecclesiology is the doctrine of the church.

2. Polity means the form of government of a church, its organizational structure.

3. Presbyterian churches, Reformed churches, Churches of Christ, Christian Churches, Brethren churches, and numerous Baptist, charismatic, and independent churches practice some form of eldership.

4. Victor A. Constien, *The Caring Elder: A Training Manual for Serving* (St. Louis: Concordia, 1986), p. 10.

5. R. Paul Stevens, *Liberating the Laity* (Downers Grove: InterVarsity, 1985), p. 147.

6. Jerome, "Letters 52," in *The Nicene and Post-Nicene Fathers*, 14 vols., Second Series, eds. Philip Schaff and Henry Wace (repr. Grand Rapids: Eerdmans, n.d.) 6:94.

7. Philip H. Towner, *1-2 Timothy & Titus*, The IVP New Testament Commentary Series (Downers Grove: InterVarsity, 1994), p. 228.

8. Jon Zens, "The Major Concepts of Eldership in the New Testament," *Baptist Reformation Review* 7 (Summer, 1978): 29.

9. Kenneth Scott Latourette, *History of Christianity*, 2 vols., 2nd ed. (New York: Harper & Row, 1975), 1: 269.

10. Ibid., 1: 261.

11. George Eldon Ladd, *A Theology of the New Testament* (Grand Rapids: Eerdmans, 1974), p. 534.

12. J. A. Motyer, *The Message of James*, The Bible Speaks Today (Downers Grove: InterVarsity, 1985), p. 189.

13. Jon Zens, "The Major Concepts of Eldership in the New Testament," *Baptist Reformation Review* 7 (Summer, 1978): 28.

14. Robert Banks, *Paul's Idea of Community* (Grand Rapids: Eerdmans, 1980), p. 53.

15. Ibid., pp. 53, 54.

16. Earl D. Radmacher, *The Question of Elders* (Portland: Western Baptist, 1977), p. 7.

17. Ibid., p. 11.

18. C. S, Lewis, "How to Get Along with Difficult People," *Eternity* 16 (August, 1965): 14.

19. Robert Greenleaf, *Servant Leadership* (New York: Paulist, 1977), p. 63.

20. Ladd, *A Theology of the New Testament*, p. 534.

21. Alfred Kuen, *I Will Build My Church*, trans. Ruby Linbald (Chicago: Moody, 1971), p. 17.

22. Ibid., p. 253.